ROMANCE
MANNERS IN MINIATURE

By the same author

Lady Behave (co-author Anne Edwards)

The English Marriage

The Bride's Book

The Art of Giving

Modern Manners

Companion volumes in the Manners in Miniature
Series previously published in paperback as
The Done Thing:

SEX (Masquerade 1996)

PARTIES (Masquerade 1996)

ROMANCE
MANNERS IN MINIATURE

Drusilla Beyfus
Cartoons by Austin

Masquerade Publications 1966

Hardback edition published in 1996 by
Masquerade Publications
Waldenbury, North Common
Chailey, East Sussex
BN8 4DR

ISBN 1 872947 05 0

A catalogue record for this book is available from
the British Library

Text revised from paperback edition (Courtship)
published by Ebury Press under the series title
The Done Thing (1992)

Designed by Jason Shulman
Manufacture coordinated in UK by Book-in-Hand Ltd
20 Shepherds Hill, London N6 5AH.

To Jason

The quotations, reprinted here with kind permission, are from: *The Pursuit of Love* by Nancy Mitford, Hamish Hamilton, 1945; *The Letters of Ann Fleming* edited by Mark Amory, Collins Harvill, 1985; *The Life of Graham Green, vol. 1* edited by Norman Sherry, Jonathan Cape, 1988. Permission to quote from Bernard Shaw's *Heartbreak House* is granted by The Society of Authors on behalf of the Bernard Shaw Estate.

Contents

Preface 1   Boy meets girl 3

Compliments 5   Flowers for you 7

Diplomatic kissing 10   Letters of love 11

Writing romance 14   Valentines 15

White lies 18   Condom etiquette 19

Canoodling 22   Rebuffs 23 ← Bought book for this useful chapter (with money saved on barge driving lessons) MAVERICK

Commiserations 25   Taxiing 27

Meet my . . . 29   The other's young 31

Fuming 33   Off the menu 36

Late excuses 38   Heavy petting 40

Apologies 43

Proposals and propositions 44

Mum's the word 47   Mr and Mrs Smith 51

Cheating 53

Preface

This book contains a little refresher course in the art of courtship. No-one doubts the universal will to pay court to the beloved, whoever he or she may be, but ways and means can always be improved upon.

The premise on which the recommendations rest is based on the power of good manners. These can be a winner's card in the right hands in wooing. Courtesy doesn't cost, carries no health risk and runs on human energy, as well as being built into the very word of courtship.

Often, when two are romantically involved, the wish to pay the other special attentions is proof of caring. In the usual scrum of life, the sexes tend to take each other for granted. Yet once a person cherishes a *tendresse* for the other, a signal sign is a willingness to go to the trouble of showing consideration.

However, it can be tricky for individuals to know how best to respond to some of the conundrums and dilemmas that beset social behaviour between the sexes in today's climate. The strict rigours of etiquette are no longer *de rigueur* in many circumstances and the chase of one for the other has a new impetus. Many of the old prescriptions about male gallantry, for example, are subject to second thoughts in the light of women's independence. And women are trying out their paces as overt initiators of togetherness between the sexes in every field from dates to sex.

Accordingly, I have highlighted a few situations that give rise to uncertainty, for which I suggest guidelines. The interpretation of courtship is liberal and is taken to mean courtship proper with a view to matrimony and when no such thought may be in the mind of either party. All sorts and conditions of romantic attachment are considered.

The recommendations suggest that good manners are their own reward but it would be unworthy not to admit to a hidden benefit. As Bernard Shaw's character Lady Utterwood in *Heartbreak House* puts it, 'if you will only take the trouble always to do the perfectly correct thing, and to say the perfectly correct thing, you can do just what you like'.

Many years on it remains a freedom all its own to know what is acceptable in a given situation.

In the interest of non-sexism,
I feel you should make the first move.

Boy meets girl

Mankind is due to colonise Venus but it doesn't get any easier to ask for a first date. Whether the chosen one would dream of going out with the proposer, or judging the moment at which to broach the question or wondering what to suggest as entertainment are issues that continue to preoccupy the human heart – post-fems and New-Age males not excepted.

Making the initial move is the famously awkward moment as few triers are free of thoughts of rebuff. Measures depend on circumstances, as a rule. Should the favourite be a virtual stranger and good manners are to be observed, a direct approach for a solo date could be thought pushy or premature. On the other hand, if the two had met before, or had mutual connections, there would seem no good reason for hanging about.

Bearing in mind that love is no respecter of conventions, a proven strategy is to allow room for manoeuvre. A direct invitation runs the risk of being turned down, a checkmate from which it is difficult to recover – for a while at any rate.

One ploy is to enlist a third party in the cause, who can propose an arrangement to which both of the couple can be invited, along with others. This last point is important as to confine numbers to the two involved can look embarrassingly like matchmaking. The point is not to make heavy weather of the presence of either party. If things go well, the prospect of proposing an initial date becomes a lot less intimidating.

A reservation is that third parties may have their work cut out if they are dealing with a slippery customer. One friend of the author's was much smitten by someone with whom he had only the briefest acquaintanceship. Extremely keen to see her again, he inveigled their mutual allies into inviting her to a succession of dos. Regularly she failed to turn up, breaking the record at the fifth try. Thereafter, wedding bells.

The amorously inclined can sail under their own colours, it goes without saying. They may send flowers. They may adopt the prerogative of hosts everywhere and invite their fancy to an occasion at which others will be present.

Women are certainly free to make the running and so do, as a matter of course. It is worth mentioning that the style of the approach matters more than the fact of it. Society expects a little more decorum from modern-day Juliets than it does from would-be Lotharios.

Compliments

It is the day of the quality compliment. Rarely have crass or tacky personal remarks between the sexes been so unfavourably looked upon.

Ideally, well-judged compliments should make the recipients feel good about themselves instantly and also contain an after-taste that can be pondered upon with satisfaction. As well, the remark should help to enhance the reputation of the payer of the praise in the eyes of the favoured.

Some people delight in extravagant praise about themselves and lap it up as if it were their due. Others, more discriminating perhaps, take a cool view of flattery that is difficult to swallow.

Question marks hover over the acceptability of certain forms of compliments paid by men to women. Doubtful choices are wolf-whistle perceptions of a woman's femininity, or comments that see her wholly in terms of her sexual potential. Admittedly, much depends on style and manner, qualities that can make desirable what in other circumstances might be viewed queasily.

It is safe to say that women like to be appreciated for their attributes as individuals. No marks for the Old Adam 'cooer' response, which may be viewed as virtual molestation by a small minority of women.

Reading the mind of the beloved is the only sure path to knowing what will specially gratify in giving praise though some leads can be gleaned from famous examples in fact and fiction. The following are declarations of love. Shakespeare's King Henry V woos his Katharine with the line, 'You have witchcraft in your lips, Kate.' The poet John Keats wrote to his beloved Fanny Brawne, thus: 'When you are in the room my thoughts never fly out of window: you always concentrate my whole senses.' In Nancy Mitford's novel *The Pursuit of Love*, her hero Fabrice declares to Linda, 'from the very first moment I knew this was as real as all the others were false, it was like recognising somebody.' The theme that the beloved transforms existence runs through many a loving declaration. James Bond's creator, the novelist Ian

Fleming, wrote this to Ann Rothermere, whom he was to marry, 'My precious, it's too extraordinary being without you. It's made everything go suddenly uninteresting.'

These are high compliments. What of the minor bouquets in conversation on a date? Almost everyone likes to have their praises sung by the favourite. Being perceptive about someone's interesting choice of apparel, or declaring that they are looking marvellous, or saying that there is no-one he or she would rather be with or vowing that the hours have dragged by until they turned up are likely to fall on receptive ground. Warmth of tone can perk up even a platitude.

Receiving compliments gracefully is also an art. You may say 'Thank you', or 'Thank you very much' or perhaps return the compliment. After which you leave it at that. The self-deprecatory wish to go into the endless reasons why you are not worthy, and so forth, of such praise, is to be resisted. It's like dissecting a butterfly.

Flowers for you

Flowers chosen for you have a special cachet. Givers of a bouquet have all sorts of ways of imbuing the gesture with particular meaning.

Taking care over the choice of flowers, bearing in mind that scent, colour and season deserve a place in deliberations, going to some trouble to write the accom-

I want a bouquet to express mild disappointment.

panying card yourself in place of relying on a ready-printed card or the anonymous hand of the flower girl are some of the means.

For part of the beauty of sending flowers is that no strings are attached. They may be sent by way of introduction, or to say thank you, or to mark a milestone or convey an apology. A bouquet sent out of the fullness of heart without formal cause can come to one and all as a wonderful surprise.

Women may send flowers to men without having their motives misinterpreted, and do. A buttonhole for an occasion is a favourite, or a bunch to cheer or embellish. The notion that only wimps would appreciate flowers has died a justifiable death.

The first flowers to herald a new season still have a place in people's affections despite the proliferation of all-the-year-round varieties. Many a heart leaps at the sight of an early bunch of sweet peas in June. A mixed bouquet has its devotees but care should be taken in selection as some ready-made mixtures consist of varieties that do not work well together when arranged in a vase. Most importantly, whatever is chosen should arrive in mint condition. To be sent a wilting bouquet is sad enough in the usual run of things. But to receive flowers from the boyfriend that are withering on the stem is particularly disappointing, and who knows, may strike a symbolic note.

An admirer can detect if his date has high expectations of receiving a flowery tribute by looking for clues in her lair. Is she over-endowed with rush baskets that once contained exotic house plants? Are the remains of rivals' bunches to be found, stalks upward, in the swing bin? Is there a plethora of vases about the place hinting that numbers are needed in which to park her flowers? In these cases it seems worth mentioning that an exuberant bouquet is rarely an inconvenience.

May one indicate disappointment through the choice of a plant? Some say it with . . . a cactus.

It's called French kissing.

Diplomatic kissing

The hand kiss may soon be with us once again. Graceful, gender specific and safe, it has none of the uncertainty that attends the sociable peck on one cheek? or both?

An import from the Continent, hand kissing is a gesture to be compared in manner and meaning to a handshake. It should be done naturally without flourishes of formality. The method is for the man to raise the woman's hand to his lips and having inclined his head, to lightly perform a kiss upon it. The woman may offer her hand, look him in the eye and once the courtesy is accomplished, withdraw it.

Who knows? This may be tomorrow's first kiss of remembrance.

Letters of love

Anyone can write a love letter if they have a mind to. There are no rules about the composition or approach, except to say your say with all the powers at your command. People who express themselves easily are at a technical advantage, no doubt, but those to whom the effort is rare and a struggle to accomplish have that factor as an arrow in their quiver.

One of the advantages of putting pen to paper is that distance between the writer and the addressed may liberate. Whatever sentiment might be awkward to utter in conversation may seem the most natural expression in the world when flowing from a pen. Also, letter writers may take advantage of total privacy.

Nevertheless a love letter is a sensitive document and every word and nuance may hold a clue for the recipient. Beginnings and endings, for example, are usually scanned first on the page by the reader as a pointer to their standing in the heart of the loved one. Invention

My darling Smoochybum – Oh, damn the spellcheck.

and imagination come into their own even in these brief lines in which affections can be epitomised and passions stated.

All is grist to the letter writer. Compliments can be paid without fear of arousing suspicions of sexist harassment. Flattery may be chanced, and as good a case as possible made out for the future of the affair.

Incidentally, the place of humdrum reminders is debatable in a love letter. Many might feel that a sudden descent into domesticity, DIY and business matters tends to lower the temperature dramatically.

If words come slowly, the fact that appearances do

count may be a source of reassurance. A well-presented letter is a particular pleasure to read and reread. Someone who has a reputation for being casual about such finer points may score by showing a willingness to take great pains.

Longed-for loving epistles are by nature read by a forgiving eye. Purists can always find an excuse for slips and errors in the writer's passion.

As a love letter is the most personal of communications, it is usually handwritten. In theory, the mere sight of the sweetheart's hand is enough to send a thrill of anticipation through the recipient. And that is the way it is, as a general rule. But what if the loved one's handwriting is virtually illegible? In this far-from-exceptional instance, there seems a good case for dispensing with the convention that holds that private correspondence rattled off on a word processor is unacceptable. The recommendation is to opt for clarity over etiquette. The letter can be topped and tailed by hand as a gesture.

Illicit love communications merit a mention as the whole history of Cupid's correspondence is steeped in secrecy. It goes without saying that it would be thoughtless and bad mannered to expose someone to the risk of embarrassment. Discretion in the use of language is advised if discovery of the letter by a third party would be contentious. In any case, a great deal of heartache might be saved if sensitive love letters were tied up in ribbons and kept out of harm's way.

My dearest darling etcetera . . .

Writing romance

A formula for a love letter being a contradiction in terms
and a heartsinker as well, none such will be given here.
Any ready-made composition would obviously destroy
the soul of a love letter, the point of which is that it
comes from the heart and hand of the beloved.
Certainly, correspondents may dip into the poets and
quote apt quotations. But there can be few recipients
who would not prefer the sentiments of the sender, even

if rough hewn or short, to a spate of borrowed felicitous expressions.

What may be usefully demonstrated, on the other hand, is the stuff of an inspiring declaration of love, illustrated below in a letter from the celebrated British novelist Graham Green to Vivien Dayrell-Browning. It reads: 'Wanted–by me, Miss Dayrell. Alias Vivien. Dear One, Darling, darling heart, marvellous wonderful, adorable one, Angel, Loveliest in the world, Sweetest Heart, Dear only love for ever, sweet one, old thing, dear desire. Description: Hair–dark and lovely, eyes grey-green and more beautiful than any other eyes; figure, perfect; complexion, wonderful; skin texture, as a rose petal; feet, very small and very adorable; disposition, sleepy. Known to her partner in crime as My Love.'

Valentines

Saint Valentine's Day on February 14th each year has become embedded in the national calendar as a wooer's festival. Like a lot of causes in Britain, the nation laughs at what it loves. The occasion is mock serious and in myth allows lovers to declare their passion under the cloak of anonymity.

With origins in classical antiquity, which have more to do with the coupling of birds than the worthy Saint, the

serenade has outlasted the cynics.

Latterly, standards have sunk or at least the core convention of anonymity has been bent. The whimsical, humorous, comical messages published in the press on Valentine's Day usually bear a pet name name best known to one little reader.

The manners of the matter are to do with avoiding causing hurt, notwithstanding that all is fair in love and on Saint Valentine's Day.

Needless to add, most people are chuffed to receive a declaration or the request 'Will you be my Valentine?', including quite grown-up persons. But what if the anonymous donor of the bunch of red roses decides to identify him or herself and the attentions are unwelcome?

That some things should be allowed to remain a mystery is a general counsel. Otherwise, the object of desire should always remember to thank for the card or flowers as a matter of courtesy, whilst simultaneously indicating that any further overtures would not go down well. Difficult as it can be to make this point within the bounds of politeness, the declinee can always state that he or she is not in the mood for romance, or a possibly more effective deterrent is an enthusiastic mention of a new emotional interest.

The rebuffed can always take refuge in the humour of Saint Valentine's Day, or claim that the gesture was for the sake of friendship only. They could argue that it is only on this occasion that one may send a bunch without risk of any heavy implications. However, experience suggests that out of hand rejection is not necessarily the last word.

Teasing the lovelorn is another topic that comes into its own on this day of misrule. The classic wheeze is for a mischievous third party to send a false declaration of adoration to the person whose affections are unrequited, in the delightful expectation that he or she will actually imagine the missive comes from the beloved. The repercussions make good plots in novels, plays and movies. In real life, as in all matters connected with affairs of the heart, it is all too easy to miscalculate the reactions of the victim, and the repercussions may take a nasty turn. One to be visited on stoics only.

The previously mentioned published Valentines put an onus on the correspondent being discreet about a public announcement. In cases where one party is cheating on a third party and there is a risk of the betrayed scanning the lines in print, it should be remembered that the drift of a sense of humour, a turn of phrase, a word even, can blow a cover as cleanly as a signature. Therefore if cheating Bear wishes to continue his/her dalliance with gallivanting Piglet, the watchword is just that.

White lies

A forgivable form of insincerity, white lies come into their own when a woman who is going out with someone wishes to demurr when a third party telephones for a date. Among the phrases that float down innumerable wires are these pale fibs that may not take anyone in but are intended to let down the inviter lightly: 'I've got someone coming from abroad.' . . . 'I've lost my diary and daren't make any plans.' . . . 'Things are a bit topsyturvy at present.' . . . 'Unfortunately, I've got a late meeting on Friday.' . . . 'I've earmarked Sunday for my young brother.' . . . 'I'd love to go out, really, sometime'.

In other words, she has a new boyfriend but she's not ready to go public yet.

Condom etiquette

Being swept off one's feet, capitulating to passion, being seduced are part of romance and all difficult to combine with handing your lover a condom.

Women seem to want to keep an element of romance and at the same time enjoy the confidence that comes from unrisky sex. The etiquette of condom-carrying is an integral element in this idealised goal.

That women would be mad not to be responsible for themselves by ensuring that male protectives are to hand in an affair in which these may be required, has been widely recognised. But acceptance of the practice has not given a lead on civilised and unembarrassing ways of managing the freedom.

As one young woman said, 'We all know it is okay to carry condoms. The tricky part is knowing exactly the right moment to produce one.' In truth, manners are in the making here.

On a first date it would be thought unseemly, very probably, for the woman to reveal that she had taken the precaution of bringing safety measures. Most would take the view that she should show some discretion about her be-preparedness. An allied topic of sensitivity are the questions that a woman may wish to put to a man about his sexual bill of health – and similarly he about hers. Again, for both partners, a sense of timing and the way

things are put can transform what might otherwise smack of a health-clinic interrogation into an expression of loving concern.

Bearing in mind the vulnerability of guidelines on matters related to sex, opinion holds that the most tactful moment for the protective to be produced is not during the arousal preliminaries but just before one is needed. On the question of retrieval, it cannot make sense to be prepared for sex and to have the means at an awkward distance from the bed or wherever. Few men would think it forward for a woman to keep her supplies somewhere where they are readily accessible – a pocket or

*There is a fine line dividing displays of
affection from foreplay.*

purse within easy reach, for example. Bags usually have
to be foraged through and have a habit of being placed
at an inconvenient distance from the excitement.

A much-needed requirement is a decorous means of
transporting protectives. Jewellery is beginning to have
its uses in this connection, though the idea is in its early
stages. Some innovative designers have made brooches
and suchlike with purpose-made compartments for protectives and pills. The beauty of these is that they enable
the wearer to be the only one in the know. The piece
might be an adornment pure and simple, or might contain a premeditated protection for the purposes of sex.

Canoodling

For lovers to want to kiss and fondle each other is only natural and no-one's concern but their own. But there are limits. Courtesy is to know where to draw the line between canoodling on a seat in the park and indulging in erotic displays of affection in public.

As a general principle of good manners is to try to avoid embarrassing others, prudery does not come into the rationale of recommending discretion. Displays of erotic arousal between human beings have long been hedged by sanctions and laws of decency but it is the lesser breaches that fall short of illegality that concern us here.

Establishing limits is difficult. People react differently; what may be thought of as offensive by some might be considered as expressions of love's young dream by others. A familiar guideline is that indoors and at close quarters is held to be more provocative than in public places. As well, it could be said that forms of love-making that caused unwitting observers to want to look away, or to feel they are intruding on a private act or to wish the amorous pair seclusion is discourteous.

It would be thoughtful if lovers kept gestures light and affectionate in public and reserved Elizabeth Barrett Browning's kisses, 'as long and silent as the night' for private delectation.

Rebuffs

In a modern version of the fairy tale, Prince Charming reverses his role and turns into the frog. His big mistake with the Princess was that he wouldn't take no for an answer.

This is not so far off rude reality. The whole question of how women can deal with an admirer who won't take a hint is highly charged in the climate of equality between the sexes. A complicating factor in suggesting guidelines is that it is partisan to consider all the many different forms and styles of overtures under one problematic barrier. Advances range from idle flirtations that can be brushed off inconsequentially to harassment that calls for heavier measures.

Watchwords in all cases, though, are detachment without resorting to discourtesy. Invitations should be thanked for and declined, any present acknowledged and returned, telephone calls deflected – a difficult one this if the pursued one doesn't wish to remain in Purdah. On the question of letters, some might hold it discourteous not to reply, and they have a point. One way round would be an acknowledgment that said that further letters would not be answered.

In general, the old etiquette that no explanations are necessary holds good, and for good reason.

I told her I was staying in to wash my hair.

Justifications run the risk of sounding defensive, may invite rebuttals and moreover, protract proceedings. Consistency is all important. Any indication of a let-up is likely to add fuel to the flame.

Despite temptations to think otherwise, it is rarely sound practice for the sought-after person to adopt contentious or provocative measures, or to let fly with insults. Brusque sexual rejection is held to be extremely disturbing to the male psyche; his reaction may be to feel his masculinity is called into question and he has to prove himself to himself. Another point in extenuation of his behaviour is that in his mind an understanding existed that had been dishonoured. In any event, whichever practical move is made, room should be allowed for face-saving. A good-humoured approach is a wonderful defuser of tension here.

Such placatory tactics are no match for a real pest. Women subject to an obsessive level of chasing should do their utmost to remain in company and avoid staying alone as a matter of course at night, and to put a male voice on the outgoing message in any answering machine, or to have telephone calls intercepted. When possible it would be a precaution for a third party to know the whereabouts of the victim most of the time.

If the thing doesn't die down, it may be necessary to consult a solicitor. In this case, chapter and verse will be asked for.

Commiserations

This piece of wisdom is for friends or allies who find themselves in the position of attempting to console the broken-hearted on a recent break-up.

Local advice depends greatly on circumstances but certain strategies on what not to do apply widely. Tactlessness as a rule is to focus on your own troubles as a means of showing the wounded they are not alone in their distress. The risk here is that they won't hear, or if they do, the fact that the helpmate's problems evidently overshadow in *gravitas* their own, may make them feel guilty about drawing attention to their tale. The other

Please feel free to say that I was too good for him.

probability is that they may resent in some way what they may see as a blind spot in you in comparing your own fracas to their emotional upheaval.

It might be as well to avoid passing value judgments in the event of any alleged misconduct by an offending party. The couple may get together again and your sentiments may redound dismally to your discredit. Another point: if there is a ghost of a hope for the future of the romance, and all else is equal, consolation calls for an optimistic appraisal of the chances of reconciliation.

Listen and listen is classic advice. The tearful should be allowed the outlet of tears without exhortations to pull themselves together.

In the outpouring of emotion material assistance may be of more use than words of comfort: a decent meal or a cash loan, or even a supply of paper tissues for appearance's sake may all help to restore a sense of well-being. The loyalty of friends is usually some compensation for loss.

Needless to add, all shared confidences call for the utmost discretion.

Taxiing

Shakespeare's King Richard III cries, 'My Kingdom for a horse!' Many have felt the same way about a taxi-cab for hire.

As taxies spell convenience, and whatever is convenient is part of showing consideration, it follows that gallantry is to allow a date the chance of a first available ride. It has been said that greater love hath no man than to pass up a free taxi-cab when cabs are as rare as a kiss in Purgatory, and he has an important meeting on the agenda too.

Taxi manners between the sexes have developed a code of their own. Courtesy is for the man to take the initiative in hailing a cab on behalf of his date. If it is a first date and he is going her way, it would be polite to

Let's compromise. I'll go to my place and you go to yours.

ask if he might accompany her. The form is to open the door so she may jump in first, to give instructions to the driver, to occupy the seat beside the woman and to close the door. At the destination, the male alights ahead of his passenger, holds the door for her and (hopefully) pays the fare.

In a trip when the woman's destination is only a short distance beyond his own, consideration is to ask the cabbie to drop her off first, and never mind the detour involved in back-tracking. A very generous act in instances when the date's journey's end is an impractical schlep from his own stop-off, is for him to advance the fare for the whole ride when he disembarks.

Amorous behaviour in the back seats of taxies has long been a topic for jokes and innuendo. On the subject: passes merit discretion if only on the grounds that any move runs the risk of being shared by passing motorists and pedestrians with a view through the windows, to say nothing of the cabbie and his mirror. The case in favour of big hats is that they may provide a decorous screen for canoodling.

Meet my . . .

'This is Nick,' says his female companion, without using a handle to denote that the person being introduced is *the* Nick, and the two are a couple.

The question of how to introduce and refer to the person whose affections have a special standing in your heart, is not easily answered. So many and varied relationships outside marriage exist and none of them have produced a workable term to describe the status of the loved one.

Terms are unsatisfactory in different ways. 'Bloke' sounds butch. 'Guy' brings to mind doll. 'Partner' suggests a business associate. 'Beau' is an archaism. 'My

That was no wife. That was my lady.

other half' has patronising undertones. 'My man' and 'My woman' strike a possessive note. 'Lover' and 'Mistress' are over-specific but interestingly they are used as signposts in general conversation with third parties.

No wonder the tendency is to hark back to the slang of the Twenties for a lighthearted solution. Still with us is 'Girlfriend' and 'Boyfriend' – best said with a touch of irony about those who have outgrown the terms.

Those who are contemplating matrimony have the old French word 'Fiancé' to rely on. It is always correct. It applies to both sexes and has a written gender distinction with advantages. Writers to the prospective bride or bridegroom may always refer to the one's 'Fiancé(e)' if the name of the intended escapes them.

The other's young

A question that buzzes in Cupid's wake has nothing to do with hitting it off with Mr Right and concerns how to get along with his children. And the same goes for a man whose girlfriend has children.

This is a field of high sensitivities besides which the classic eternal triangle is a simple equation. Few problems about children admit of easy solutions. One fact seems to be that a pre-condition of success is the cooperation and understanding of the third party, and his or her willingness to accept the other's children as a priority in their own arrangements.

Danger zones concern unwanted attempts by the quasi-step-parent to step into the shoes of the children's biological one. Disciplining tiresome youngsters brings this to a head. An approach that is likely to go down well when reported to the absent parent is less along the lines of 'I told you not to . . .' and more 'Your mother wouldn't approve . . .'

On visits it goes without saying that punctuality and reliability about arrangements is more than usually important, as is keeping any promise about treats and anticipated excursions. During these encounters many a parent's lover has discovered the wisdom of keeping intimacies in a low key or at least until the relationship comes closer to being accepted by the small fry.

It's all right to try to buy my affection.

Details may carry great weight. One girlfriend of a man with two growing boys took great care about giving them nice presents and was careful to present the offerings in her own name only and not to attempt a surrogate 'mother and father' gesture – a point that was liked by the children whose own mother had kept up the custom of giving presents in the name of herself and the children's father.

When matrimony is planned between a couple with children of an age from a previous marriage, a way of introducing the prospective step-parent is for the party to go off on holiday together.

Fuming

The smoking debate is hot enough in the usual run of events. Add a romance between an 'anti' and a habitual dragger on the weed and goodwill between the two is liable to be burnt out.

Presupposing a wish to please, what part may courtesy play in the action? The sensitive area consists of the situations, occasions and circumstances when smoking is still a matter of personal discretion. Smoking may be prohibited in most public places but this fails to take account of restaurants, certain international air flights, the street and life at home. As usual, points have to be stretched, allowances made and the benefit of the doubt given if politeness and peace are to prevail.

Abstainers could show willing by occupying seats or spaces where smoking is permitted instead of opting for separation or togetherness on his or her terms. Furthermore, they might make exceptions and display a generous tolerance of their companion's wish to light up at table or in rooms in which smokers may puff away. Tact could be shown about not remonstrating in public – especially in front of parents or friends. A delicate topic that requires diplomacy is the approach to any off-putting physical manifestations of the habit such as whiffy breath and nicotine-stained finger nails – a good tip for a spring clean might be more effective than criti-

cism. Above all, the person on the side of the angels could try to soft-pedal the worn-in-the-groove litany of the need to kick the habit whilst not losing any opportunity to subtly encourage any attempts to give up.

Puffers, for their part, can endeavour to control the vexation caused to others by their foible. In practical terms, they can exhale smoke tactfully. Falling ash, cigarette butts and all the paraphernalia of smoking can be managed tidily or messily. Windows can be opened in smoke-filled rooms, if necessary. Ashtrays can be emptied on departure. It would also be considerate for them to attempt to bring a sufficiency of supplies to any gathering as the need to beg, borrow or steal a smoke is an irksome reminder of dependency. Above all, smokers could show mercy and refrain from reiterating all the familiar arguments for the defence: that restrictions are an infringement of personal liberty, their detractor's foibles are nastier in comparison and that dear old uncle Ben, who lived to ninety, was a two-pack-a-day man. Clearly, the supreme conciliatory act is to cut down on the consumption of tobacco.

Among the changes in smokers' manners between the sexes is the demise of a favourite masculine device for striking up an acquaintance with a stranger. It was much featured in old movies: our hero, stranded in at some inhospitable bus stop or bar or railway station, espies a beautiful stranger who is raising an unlit ciggie to her lips. A flash of flame, and the plot advances. Should a male attempt this in rude reality in a public place, he runs the risk of having his motives questioned. At a private party, he could always try his luck with the proviso that he refrains from making too much of a production of the politeness.

Long considered polite behaviour for a man escorting a woman who smokes tobacco is to carry cigarettes, to offer her one before helping himself, to light her smoke before his own and to attempt to locate an ashtray for her comfort if none is handy.

I'm sure that chef will be delighted to provide a calorie count, Madam.

Off the menu

Dieters on dates have their work cut out if Sparta is not to conquer Athens. The conflict of interests peaks on occasions when dieters have a special wish to make a success of the occasion.

Regime watchers know all too well there is no wholly happy resolution to this dilemma. Even blowing the diet may have unhappy consequences in the long term with loss of will power, failure to stick to the discipline and ballooning developments leading to loss of the dear one.

A tactic that works is to maintain the appearance of things by dissembling. Dieters may play down unsociable gestures of refusal through a mixture of pretence and cunning.

In place of declining a first course, they may order a little something that can be nibbled appreciatively and the remainder left uneaten. If this is done it will spare healthy eaters the choice of being obliged to eat alone or of adopting the spartan ways of their companion. A measure is to make one course into two – a satisfactory dieter's equation sometimes – by ordering the dish to be served in two parts: an accompaniment on a side dish such as a vegetable could serve as a starter with the main ingredient ordered to follow.

When wine is poured, a more hospitable reaction than placing a hand strictly over the mouth of the glass, is to accept a little of the grape. The very spectacle of a companion's unfilled glass is gloomy to many imbibers; drinking on your own offends a basic code of hospitality. Besides, should abstainers maintain their resolve, drinkers can look forward to downing a reserve drop or two when their own glass is empty.

Other compromises can be rallied to the cause. Half portions of dishes can be ordered without risk of giving offence (except perhaps to the chef). Ingredients can be asked for shorn of the proscribed elements, with the proviso that the ordering stage doesn't turn into a dietary seminar.

Love birds also have the advantages of being able to share a course: one pudding and two spoons is the prerogative of lovers.

Late excuses

When Tardy steps out with Punctuality, mollifying tactics are likely to be in order. Those with the habit of being in good time may, or may not, adjust to keeping company with a belated beloved.

Unpunctuality suggests to many that the company that awaits is taken for granted. Avoidable lateness is thought of as a sign of selfishness.

The question to be addressed here is how might latecomers excuse themselves with honour? Gender, location and their role on the occasion all have a bearing on the answer.

Par for the course is that a contrite face is worth a thousand justifications. The belated one might also spare the awaiting company the usual fictions by way of explanation. The likelihood is they will not believe a word when the excuses are trotted out to them, so it might be an idea to forgo the easy way out. Traffic jams, being kept late at work, a sudden dearth of taxies, a herd of cows on the lane: all may be accurate but as explanations they have long lost their credibility.

Instead, it would be a compliment to the company either to add some believable detail to the tale or to indulge in creative apologies. Who could resist the excuse proffered by an acquaintance of the author's whose justification for appalling lateness at her boyfriend's party was that she had been detained by her father's centipede. It was her day for feeding, she volunteered. As it happened, she was speaking the truth, but who cared?

Lateness calls for apologies the degree of which depends on circumstances. A sliding scale related to the duration of the lapse might go along the following lines, on the basis that it was a special occasion.

Ten minutes behind schedule – perfunctory apologies if the person is a guest, stated regrets if he or she is the host for not being on hand for greeting.

Fifteen to twenty minutes late – a considered apology and a convincing excuse (see above).

Thirty minutes after the appointed hour – profound apologies and genuine contrition. The cause of the belatedness is not the point; the inconvenience, annoyance and maybe anxiety is.

A factor that has a bearing on the politeness of putting in a punctual appearance concerns the nature of the meeting spot and the sex of the person who awaits. If this is to be in a public place, there is an onus on the male to see that his date is not left unaccompanied for long. This is particularly so when meeting in a public house. Whereas women frequent bars on their own if they so wish, perceptions change when they are out on a date. In any case, it is nice to be greeted on arrival with 'What will you have?'

Heavy petting

A classic instance of a passion killer is a clash of loyalties on the matter of canines as house pets. Suppose someone who doesn't care for dogs – not to put too fine a point on it – falls for one who shares his or her life with an adored canine. What sort of concessions are likely to win over the doggy one, bearing in mind the force of St Bernard's proverb, 'Love me, love my dog'?

In aiming to please, it is as well to remember that dog lovers as a breed appreciate any kindness that is shown to their animal, and are correspondingly dismayed by acts that betray a lack of sympathy for canines in general and their house pet in particular.

Dissenters can always make an honourable exception in the case of their date's animal, and try to establish friendly relations. It can be risky to overdo overtures. Animals are famously sensitive to false bonhomie. A tip

It's his way of making you welcome.

might be that if chocolate drops are permitted by the owner, don't miss out on a round.

If the dog is kept in a city, it would be considerate for whoever is proposing a date to ask if the canine's owner would like to bring his or her animal, and to bear in mind the needs of the pet when making arrangements. It is wisest to check first with the animal's owner before embarking on plans involving periods of separation between hound and keeper, or visits to friends' houses where canines are kept. Offers to dog-sit would probably be thought generous, as would including the canine in any invitation to a country weekend. And any willingness to take the hound on a healthy ramble would win approval, with bonus points for not chickening out of the offer on a wet and windy day.

Presents for the hound – be these practical or playful – would probably carry more weight than an offering intended for the owner. Good snapshots of the canine are likely to be treasured whether the owner occupies the frame or not.

A whiff of partisanship may be in order if the hound gets into a scrap. As a witness with undoggy credentials, it may be obligatory to be economical with the truth, if the account of who growled first is to be believed by the dog's owner.

Canine owners may draw a parallel between the attitude of someone to their hound and the character of that person. An encouraging factor for the would-be beloved is that the dog lover may correlate any acceptance of the hound's quirks with a preparedness to match this with a tolerance of the shortcomings of the hound's owner.

A point in mitigation of previously voiced criticism of canines might be the fact of not having had a chance to own a dog in childhood. To dog lovers, this might be barking up the right tree.

It should be said that in order to make the compromises worthwhile in the above cases, one party has to be truly exceptional.

I suspect that I may have done something to
arouse your displeasure . . .

Apologies

The old adage 'Never apologise, never explain' is poor
counsel to the romantically inclined. Explanations as
part of justifications for untoward behaviour and apologies are balm of particular value during the stage when
two people are getting to know one another. A willingness to express regrets for what was done or undone can
help to mend and ameliorate.

The point of an apology is that it makes public the

wish to make amends. The gesture may be spoken, written or come wrapped in some conciliatory move best read by the offended against. The sooner an apology is said or acted upon the better. A prompt admission indicates remorse, and, moreover may quell rising feelings of annoyance in the breast of the injured party.

Letters can be short and to the point. If words come hard, writing 'My apologies', or 'Please forgive me' or 'I am truly sorry' will convey the essential thought; grovelling is rarely sound practice.

The wish to say sorry can take many forms other than spelling it out. Those who have caused offence but who perhaps are reluctant to admit to the fact, might atone for their behaviour by offering flowers, or a present or undertaking some irksome task on behalf of the beloved.

An apology puts an end to the matter, at least until the next time.

Proposals and propositions

A proposal of marriage is a big moment for the human heart. Hopes of future happiness, fears of rejection, a sense of personal fate in the making are all concentrated in the question, 'Will you marry me?'

I want you to be my party of the second part.

People propose in as many different circumstances as there are proposals. Some do it according to the book beneath the light of the silvery moon, many are moved to pop the question in a lover's embrace in bed, some choose the least expected moment or situation in which to plight their troth. Writing a proposal of marriage on a gift tag, proposing to a loved one live on air in a radio programme and proposing daily for over a year were among the findings of a recent survey on the theme.

As people are known to remember every detail of a

proposal for forever and a day, the case for stage managing the occasion is persuasive. This doesn't have to follow conventional lines but would benefit from being somewhere that is relatively private, peaceful and allows the parties to be able to read each other's faces. It is also worth reminding the proposer that romance is how a word is put as well as what is declared.

Before matrimony is sealed a question must be put and acceptance received, which leads us to the all-too prevalent oblique proposal. A remark is made by one party that is taken by the other to imply that marriage is in the offing without any direct proposal being made. It is kind to advise those in this position to clear the air, even at the risk of embarrassment. They may adopt a similar ploy and make some remark to the effect that no such understanding exists on their side, and see if the reaction is one of dismay.

If a proposal of marriage is longed for, it should be accepted on the spot, pronto, prontissimo. No-one is obliged to give an answer immediately though. But if an assent is won, it should be meant. Sincerity is of the essence in this rite for both parties.

How to say 'No' without hurting is a difficult one. He or she might say that they know they would never be[8] able to make the person happy, or that they would rather die than see their love affair dwindle into matter-of-fact marriage. That you just don't want to get married, is reason enough.

Women do propose marriage quite frequently, with many a happy outcome. But those who do so run a double risk, of being turned down as a spouse, and being frowned upon as a proposer.

In future, managing prenuptial contracts may deserve a place alongside proposals. Knowing how to ride the horses of romance and legality simultaneously seems likely to call for a supreme balancing act. Manners are still in the embryonic phase here.

Mum's the word

The betrothed who is invited to dine for the first time with their prospective in-laws does well to remember that often, it is what is not done or said that plays as important a part in ensuring the success of the day as what is.

In general, the occasion is one on which everyone wants to do the right thing but there is a tension in the air. Generally parents don't want to seem unnaturally formal or judgmental. The son or daughter of the house wishes to present their beloved in a good light. The new member hopes to be accepted for himself or herself and has to strike a balance between the artificial postures of Best Behaviour and being mindlessly relaxed.

A few reminders. Get there on time, especially if word

has gone ahead that you are tardy by nature. Allow a few minutes grace past the appointed hour in order to allay giving the impression that you are neurotically punctilious. On the vexed question of whether to bring a bottle – probably not on this occasion. Many hosts prefer to be seen to be the sole providers on important family occasions and moreover, closer acquaintanceship may prevent the choice of an unwelcome tipple.

Don't take domestic arrangements wholly for granted. It is always considerate to offer to help the hosts and if declined, should be abided by. This doesn't mean a licence for a blind eye, however, and unobtrusive ways of lending a hand should not be ignored. If the offer is accepted, on the other hand, it is no bad idea to ask the hosts how they would like the task accomplished; many an unseemly fracas has broken out over ways of mixing a salad dressing or methods of washing up.

Politeness, as ever, is for guests to accept the customs of the house with good grace especially if these are very different from the ways things are done at home. Nevertheless, guests have privileges too, and there seems no sound case for not indicating dissent so long as this is done diplomatically. The son or daughter of the house has a role to play in circumstances in which there is a taste gap between the generations through advance briefing. Knowing what to expect helps to subvert any looming embarrassment.

Attitudes towards smoking tobacco, drink and meat-

Do try not to look like the sort of woman I'll become, Mother.

eating are divisive at many tables. It shouldn't be a counsel of perfection to recommend that on this occasion, the benefit of the doubt be given to the hosts. In any case, should a dish be served that is uncongenial for one reason or another to the newcomer, the matter may be made light of by him or her, a healthy helping of an ingredient that is to their liking indulged in and compliments to the cook.

Doing some homework on the parents' likes and dislikes, interests, hobbies, passions and predilections will not only repay effort, as a general rule, but will oil the wheels of conversation. It is worth mentioning that the parental generation usually likes to be considered as individuals by their offspring's contemporaries and not looked upon as extensions of their progeny.

This initiation rite is characterised by a sensation of skating on thin ice beneath which taboo topics await. An avoidance of leading questions on sensitive issues is only common sense. Should any awkward points be raised, some remark along the lines that they had wanted to talk about this but could it wait?, might deflect further exploration of the subject.

Very probably, the 'sizing up' of the prospective family member, which is part and parcel of the ritual, will be as much determined by the manner in which the betrothed behave towards each other as by anything else that takes place. Expressions of love and devotion can only be reassuring to civilised parents with their offspring's interests at heart. How far bantering and teasing between the couple has a place is a matter of conjecture. As a rule, even the sort of deprecating remarks that are not intended to be taken seriously are best reserved for another day.

The hour of departure: if a prompt exit is contemplated it might be tactful for the younger generation to establish the hour at which they intended to take their leave. This would afford them the chance to stay a little longer than they planned with its implications that they are having a good time.

Afterwards, with luck, all the parties can breathe a sigh of relief and thank their lucky stars that nothing went wrong.

A thank-you letter is a must.

Mr and Mrs Smith

The subterfuge that once invariably accompanied an illicit weekend in an hotel is now a matter of personal choice only, more often than not. Guilty conscience aside, little discomfiture is likely to surround a couple who are not married, or not married to each other, in this well-worn escape from propriety. The equally well-worn exception is any likelihood of being rumbled by the legal partner, or bumping into someone the escapees know.

The names under which the couple book in is the nub of the matter. In the usual course of events, the man fills in the hotel registration form, and, as a rule, no questions are asked about the name of his companion. If a woman wishes to be booked in under her own name, she will be addressed as such by the staff. Staying under an assumed name is a conventional ruse for a couple, which undoubtedly helps to explain the number of Mr and Mrs Smiths on the lips of hoteliers.

It is not unknown for a woman to feel the loss of a

Our name is Smith, so it's less embarrassing to pretend that we're not married.

band of gold in the hotel foyer, despite the atmosphere of professional acceptance. She may juggle the jewellery she is wearing, if need be.

What is considerate is for whoever makes the hotel reservation to consult the other in advance about his or her wishes on identity, and not to go ahead unilaterally.

An escort is advised to show some tact about the

choice of a hotel as a love nest. It is not necessarily to his advantage to be greeted by the management as a habitué ('Will it be your usual bottle, Sir?'). His companion may gain the distinct impression she is one of a parade.

When the time comes for settling the bill, it can happen that the name on the charge card or cheque does not tally with that in which the room was booked. An odd look from the desk is a likely reaction, but no more. What may cause shock, however is the deceiver's act of reneging on paying up. Unfortunately, he has only a cheque book on his wife's joint account and would she be a darling and use her Amex?

Cheating

Fewer souls nowadays fall for the admonition, 'Do not adultery commit;/Advantage seldom comes of it.' Cheating on the legal partner will always be with us, like gambling.

A question that crops up continually in the debate is the moment at which the parties should declare their hand on the matter of their marital status. Received wisdom on the subject – with the wish not to cause hurt in mind – is sooner rather than later.

Should the facts come as a painful surprise to one member, the procrastinating party may expect trouble –

if real-life evidence and a whole literature about betrayal is to be believed.

Nevertheless, the manner of the telling may help to soften the blow and engender a more favourable mood in the Other. The guilty party will choose a moment when his or her sweetheart is in a receptive frame of mind and, if any deception has been involved, apologise unreservedly.

Decisions on where the tale is to be told may also have an effect, one way or the other, on reactions. A deceiver's charter would probably recommend a discreetly placed table in the beloved's favourite restaurant, in preference to total privacy. Few are prepared to make a scene in public.

A reminder of the Seventh Commandment in a book on courtship would have seemed out of place to readers in the past. By definition, courting was done by those eligible for matrimony. But who will cast the first stone today? So many approaches between the sexes deserve the name of courtship, whether marriage is a possibility or not.

Forgiveness and reconciliation is always in fashion for the offended against party. And there is the possibility of fun making up.